GREAT GRAPHS
AND
SENSATIONAL
STATISTICS

Also in the Magical Math series

Dazzling Division

Delightful Decimals and Perfect Percents

Fabulous Fractions

Groovy Geometry

Marvelous Multiplication

Measurement Mania

Magical Math

GREAT GRAPHS
AND
SENSATIONAL
STATISTICS

Games and Activities
That Make Math Easy and Fun

Lynette Long

WILEY

John Wiley & Sons, Inc.

Copyright © 2004 by Lynette Long. All rights reserved
Illustrations copyright © 2004 by Tina Cash-Walsh. All rights reserved

Published by John Wiley & Sons, Inc., Hoboken, New Jersey
Published simultaneously in Canada

Design and production by Navta Associates, Inc.

The publisher and the author have made every reasonable effort to ensure that the experiments and activities in this book are safe when conducted as instructed but assume no responsibility for any damage caused or sustained while performing the experiments or activities in the book. Parents, guardians, and/or teachers should supervise young readers who undertake the experiments and activities in this book.

For general information about our other products and services, please contact our Customer Care Department within the United States at (800) 762-2974, outside the United States at (317) 572-3993 or fax (317) 572-4002.

Wiley also publishes its books in a variety of electronic formats. Some content that appears in print may not be available in electronic books. For more information about Wiley products, visit our Web site at www.wiley.com.

Library of Congress Cataloging-in-Publication Data:

Long, Lynette.
 Great graphs and sensational statistics : games and activities that make math easy and fun / Lynette Long.
  p. cm. — (Magical math)
 Includes index.
 ISBN 0-471-21060-9 (pbk.)
  1. Graphic methods—Study and teaching (Elementary) 2. Mathematical statistics—Study and teaching (Elementary) 3. Games in mathematics education. I. Title.

QA90.L586 2004
372.7—dc21   2003053456

Printed in the United States of America

10 9 8 7 6 5 4 3 2 1

Contents

I. The Magic of Graphs and Statistics   1

II. Pictographs   3

    1   But First . . . A Brief Commercial Break   5
    2   3-D Candy Pictograph   8
    3   Basketball Pictograph   11
    4   Dangling Spoons   13
    5   Television Pictograph   15

III. Bar Graphs   17

    6   Roll Them Bones   19
    7   Predict It   22
    8   Birthday Bars   24
    9   Bouncing Balls   28
    10   Pet Survey   30

IV. Pie Charts   33

    11   Just Desserts   35
    12   Flipping Coins   38
    13   Shoes . . . Shoes . . . Shoes   40
    14   Tic-Tac-Toed   43
    15   Color Feud   45

V. Line Graphs   47

    16   Grassy Lines   49
    17   Bouncing Lines   52
    18   Stock Market   55
    19   Watching Your Weight   57
    20   Temperature Tracking   60
    21   Graphy Diagrams   62

VI. Map Charts   65

    22   Family Travel   67
    23   Mail Call   69
    24   Around the World   72
    25   Weather Bingo   75

VII. All about Graphs and Charts   77

    26   Graphing Comparisons   79
    27   Scavenger Hunt   81
    28   Who Done It?   83
    29   Word Search   86

VIII. Statistics   89

    30   Mean Solitaire   91
    31   Matching Means   93
    32   Estimating Means   95
    33   GPA   97
    34   Tower Tallies   99
    35   Highest Median   102
    36   Hit the Target   104
    37   Sleep Study   106
    38   Baby Weight   108
    39   Number Memory   111
    40   Rank Order   114

Graphs and Statistics Master Certificate   116

Index   117

1

THE MAGIC OF GRAPHS AND STATISTICS

It's hard to get through a day without seeing a graph or chart somewhere, whether you're reading a newspaper or a magazine, watching an ad on television, or looking at a display in the grocery store. Graphs and charts are used everywhere because they make data easy to understand.

In this book, you are going to learn about five types of charts and graphs: pictographs, bar graphs, pie charts, line graphs, and map charts. Different types of graphs are often used to show different types of data. Pictographs are made out of pictures and have instant visual impact. Bar graphs are made up of either vertical or horizontal bars and are often used to show performance. Pie charts use sectioned circles to emphasize comparisons. Line graphs use horizontal, vertical, and diagonal lines and are especially good for tracking changes over time. Map charts use maps of a state, a country, the world, or any part of the world to make geographical comparisons.

You'll also learn a lot about statistics, which is the science of representing or grouping data so that they are easily understood. It can sound complicated, but really it's not. When you find your average test score on your spelling tests, you have computed a statistic. Instead of calling it the average, you'll call it the mean. You'll learn how to compute other statistics, too, such as the mode, median, and range. You'll learn what the normal curve is, how to tell the difference between percent and percentile, and how to rank order a group of numbers.

Most of all, learning about graphing and statistics is fun! In the activities in this book, you'll dangle a spoon on your nose, bounce different-size balls, roll dice, organize shoes, grow grass, track the mail, test the memory of your friends, do a sleep study, and much more. Why not get started? You'll be surprised how graphing and statistics will help you understand the world around you.

~~~ II ~~~

PICTOGRAPHS

Pictographs are graphs using picture-symbols. Usually, the symbol looks like the thing that you are graphing, and the number of symbols corresponds to the number of whatever you are graphing. Pictographs are fun to look at and easy to interpret.

In this part, you will make a 3-dimensional (3-D) pictograph using hard candies, track television commercials, shoot free throws with your friends, dangle a spoon from your nose, and interpret the amount of TV watched.

1

But First...A Brief Commercial Break

Before you start graphing data, you have to collect them and organize them. Try this activity to practice gathering data.

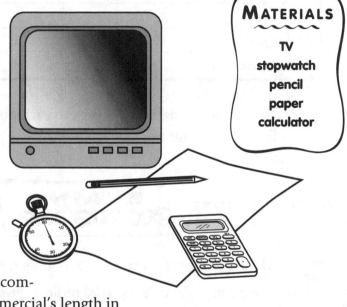

Procedure

1. Gather your materials and watch a 30-minute television show. As soon as the show starts, use the stopwatch to time the length of each commercial that you see. Make a list of the type of product each commercial advertises and the commercial's length in seconds.

EXAMPLE

soda commercial	30 seconds
credit-card commercial	60 seconds

2. Now reorganize the data by type of product. Make a list of all of the different products you recorded in the left-hand column of the chart. Use slash marks to represent the number of commercials you recorded for each product.

5

Product	Slash Marks	Tally	Total Time
Soda	/	1	
Cars	///	3	
Fast Foods	//	2	
Toys	─H̶H̶T̶ ///	8	
TV Shows	//	2	
Clothes and Shoes	////	4	
Total Commercials		20	

3. Count the number of slash marks next to each product. Enter these numbers in the "Tally" column.

BRAIN Stretcher

Record the number of commercials in three different half-hour television programs. What is the total airtime devoted to commercials over all three shows? What percentage of the airtime was devoted to commercials in each of the shows?

Now record the length in seconds of each commercial in three different hour-long television programs. What is the total time devoted to commercials? What percentage of airtime was devoted to commercials in each of the shows?

Is the same percentage of airtime devoted to commercials in both half-hour and 1-hour television programs?

4. Compute the total time of the commercials for each type of product and enter it in the last column. Add up the times in this column to get the total commercial time during the show. How many minutes of commercials were in the half hour of TV

that you watched? Which type of product had the most commercial time?

Tips and Tricks

To compute percentage of airtime devoted to commercials:

1. Find the total number of seconds used for commercials.
2. Find the total number of seconds in the program including commercials by multiplying the length of the show in minutes by 60.
3. To find the percentage, divide step 1 by step 2 and multiply the answer by 100.

Example

The total time of commercials during a 30-minute program is 600 seconds. The total time of the program (including the commercials) is 30 minutes, or 1,800 seconds. The percentage of the show devoted to commercials is 600/1,800, or 1/3 (expressed as a decimal = .333). Now we multiply this by 100 to get 33.3%.

3-D Candy Pictograph

A pictograph uses pictures to represent objects. In this activity, you're going to use candies to make a 3-dimensional (3-D) pictograph, then copy it on graph paper to make a 2-dimensional pictograph.

MATERIALS

a roll of hard candies of different colors

cardboard

glue

marker

graph paper

colored pencils

Procedure

1. Open a roll of hard candies.

2. Sort the candy pieces by color. How many candies are there of each color?

3. Line up the candies on the piece of cardboard in horizontal rows by color. Glue each row onto the cardboard. At the top of the graph, use the marker to write the title of your graph, such as "Candy Colors."

	CANDY COLORS			
Red	O	O	O	
Green	O	O	O	O
Yellow	O			
Purple	O			
Orange	O	O		

Hard Candies

4. Copy the pictograph on a sheet of graph paper using the colored pencils. Place your title at the top of the graph. At the bottom of the graph, indicate the scale for the graph. For example, one red circle = one red candy.

CANDY COLORS				
Red	●	●	●	
Green	●	●	●	●
Yellow	●			
Purple	●			
Orange	●	●		

● = one red candy
● = one green candy
● = one yellow candy
● = one purple candy
● = one orange candy

Open another roll of hard candies. Write the number of candies of each color on a sheet of paper. Put all the candies in a paper lunch bag. What is the chance of picking a red candy from the bag? Pick one candy out of the bag. What color is it? Eat it. Now that you have eaten one candy, what is the chance of picking a red candy? Pick a second candy out of the bag. Eat it. Now what is the chance of picking a red candy out of the bag?

Tips and Tricks

To figure out the chance of picking a red candy from the bag, count the number of red candies in the bag. Now count the total number of candies in the bag, including red candies. Divide the number of red candies by the total number of candies in the bag. Multiply the answer by 100. This is the chance of picking a red candy out of the bag.

3 Basketball Pictograph

Try this activity to make a record of basketball free throws for you and your friends.

MATERIALS

paper
pencil
basketball
basketball hoop
basketball stickers or star stickers
group of friends

Procedure

1. Copy the chart below on a sheet of paper.

Player	Free Throws

2. Go to a basketball court with a group of friends. Take a basketball, the chart, and the stickers with you.

3. Have the players take turns shooting free throws. Give each player a chance to shoot 10 free throws. Each time a player makes a free throw, he or she should place a sticker on the row that is marked with his or her name.

4. When everyone has finished putting on their stickers, you will have a pictograph of the group's free throws. Put a title at the top of the graph and the date at the bottom.

Player	Free Throws
Brian	🏀 🏀
John	🏀 🏀
Alice	🏀 🏀 🏀 🏀
Gwen	🏀 🏀 🏀

BRAIN Stretcher

WHAT'S YOUR FAVORITE SPORT?

Try making a pictograph of something you do in that sport, such as

- number of types of hits you make during a baseball game (singles, doubles, triples, and home runs)
- soccer goals scored by members of your team over a single season
- laps you do during swimming practice

4

Dangling Spoons

Learn to create and interpret pictographs by playing a silly spoon game and graphing the results.

MATERIALS

5 spoons
stopwatch
paper
pencil
5 volunteers

Procedure

1. Give a clean, dry spoon to each volunteer. Have the volunteers breathe hot air on the inside of their spoons and dangle the spoons from the tips of their noses.

2. As soon as a spoon is dangling, time how long it stays on the person's nose. Give each volunteer three attempts and record his or her longest score.

3. Graph each of your five volunteers' scores using a pictograph. Use a picture of one spoon to represent 2 seconds and

a picture of half a spoon to represent 1 second. Your graph should look something like this:

Nosey Spoons

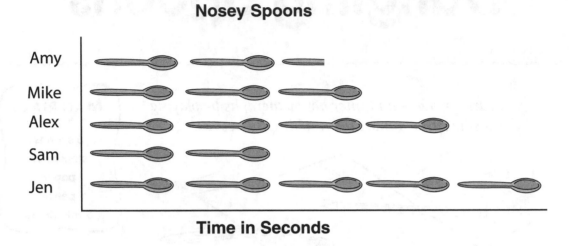

Time in Seconds

 = 2 Seconds

4. Look at the finished graph and answer the following questions: Who had the longest time according to your graph? Who had the shortest? What was the difference between the longest time and the second longest time? How would this difference be represented in spoons?

14

Television Pictograph

Read a pictograph and answer questions about the data it represents. Then have a contest with the people in your family to see who can watch the least TV.

MATERIALS

graph paper
colored
pencils
pencil

Procedure

1. This pictograph uses pictures to show how many hours of TV one student watches per day over the course of 1 week. Look at the graph and answer the following questions on a piece of paper:

	Hours of Television Watched
Monday	▨
Tuesday	
Wednesday	▨ ◤
Thursday	▨
Friday	▨ ◤
Saturday	▨ ▨ ◤
Sunday	▨ ▨

▨ = 1 hour

15

On which day did the student watch the most TV?

On which day did the student watch the least TV?

What was the average amount of TV that the student watched during a single day of the week? What was the average amount of TV that the student watched on a single weekend day?

If the student had a TV curfew of 2 hours a day, on how many days did the student go over the curfew?

How many total hours of television did the student watch during the week?

2. Have a contest with the members of your family. See who can watch the least television in a single week. Make a pictograph of each person's television viewing. Use a different-colored pencil for each person's graph. Add to the graphs each day. Who won the contest at the end of the week?

BRAIN Stretcher

What if each picture of a television in the above graph represented 2 hours of TV watched? Answer the same questions from the exercise and see how this affects your answers.

III

BAR GRAPHS

Aries: March 21 - April 19

Taurus: April 20 - May 20

Gemini: May 21 - June 20

Cancer: June 21 - July 22

Leo: July 23 - August 22

Virgo: August 23 - September 22

Libra: September 23 - October 22

Scorpio: October 23 - November 21

Sagittarius: November 22 - December 21

Capricorn: December 22 - January 19

Aquarius: January 20 - February 18

Pisces: February 19 - March 20

The Zodiac Wheel

Bar graphs are one of the most common ways of displaying data. They make it easy to compare different things, such as the number of times something happens or the percentage of people who answered yes to a certain question. Bar graphs can be displayed either horizontally or vertically. They are easy to design and easy to read.

In this part, you will look at the chance of rolling certain numbers with dice, discover the zodiac signs of your family and friends, experiment with ball bouncing, and survey the pet preferences of your friends. At the same time, you will learn all about bar graphs!

Roll Them Bones

Learn something about chance while constructing a bar graph.

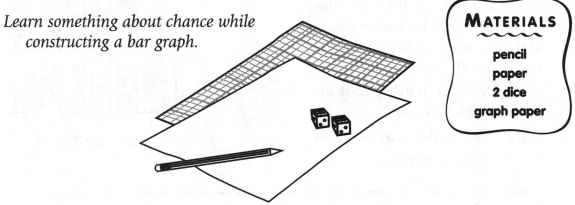

Procedure

1. Make a copy of the chart below on a piece of paper.

Number Rolled	Slash Marks	Total
One		
Two		
Three		
Four		
Five		
Six		

2. Roll one die 36 times. After each roll of the die, enter a slash mark next to the number that you just rolled (in the second column of the chart).

3. After you've done all 36 rolls, count the total number of slash marks for each number and put the results in the third column of the chart.

4. Enter the results in a bar graph. Put the numbers you could roll—1, 2, 3, 4, 5, and 6—on the horizontal axis. Put the number of times you rolled each number on the vertical axis. Label each axis and give your graph a title. Now enter your data by creating bars that extend from the number rolled on the horizontal axis up to the amount of times this number was rolled. (It helps to use a ruler to make your lines straight.) Look at this graph as a model:

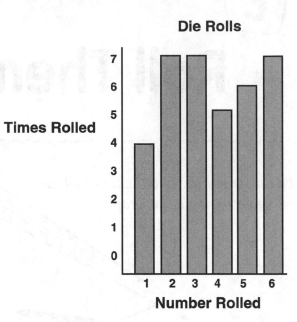

5. Make a copy of the chart below on another piece of paper.

Number Rolled	Slash Marks	Total
One		
Two		
Three		
Four		
Five		
Six		
Seven		
Eight		
Nine		
Ten		
Eleven		
Twelve		

6. Now roll a pair of dice 36 times. The numbers that can be rolled are 2, 3, 4, 5, 6, 7, 8, 9, 10, 11, and 12.

7. After each roll of the two dice, add up the numbers showing on the dice and make a slash mark in the second column of the chart next to the number you rolled.

8. Count the total number of slash marks for each number and put the results in the third column of the chart. How many of each number were rolled?

9. Enter the results in a bar graph. Put the numbers you could roll—2, 3, 4, 5, 6, 7, 8, 9, 10, 11, and 12—on the horizontal axis. Put the number of times you rolled each number on the vertical axis. Label each axis and give your graph a title. Now enter your data by creating bars that extend from the number rolled on the horizontal axis up to the amount of times this number was rolled. Look at this graph as a model:

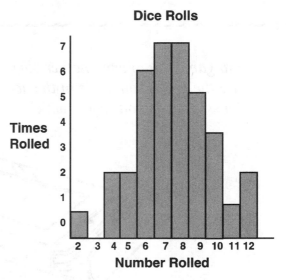

10. Compare the two graphs. Why do you think they look different?

BRAIN Stretcher

Using two dice, how many ways are there to roll each of the numbers 2 through 12? For example, there are three ways to roll the number 4: you could roll 3 and 1, 1 and 3, or 2 and 2. Graph the number of possibilities for each number. How does this graph compare to the graph you made from rolling the two dice?

Predict It

In this card game, try to win another player's cards by rolling dice. Use the graph you made in the activity "Roll Them Bones" to help you choose which cards to play.

MATERIALS

playing cards
2 dice
2 players

Game Preparation

Remove the aces and the kings from a deck of playing cards.

Game Rules

1. Deal each player five cards. Place the remaining cards facedown in the center of the table.

2. Each player chooses one card from his or her hand and places it faceup on the table.

3. Player 1 rolls the dice. If the sum of the numbers rolled matches the number on any of the playing cards that are faceup, player 1 wins both cards. If not, both cards stay on the table. Jacks represent 11 and queens represent 12.

4. Both players draw a new card from the stack of cards in the center of the table so that each player holds five cards. Each player selects one card from his or her hand to place faceup on the table. Player 2 rolls both dice. If the sum of the numbers rolled matches any of the playing cards that are faceup, then player 2 wins all the cards on the table.

5. Play continues until there are no more cards in the center of the table. The player with the most cards wins the game.

Tips and Tricks

As you play, look back at your "Roll Them Bones" graph and ask yourself these questions:

Which numbers are easiest to roll with two dice?

Which numbers are hardest to roll?

Which cards should you put down when it is your turn to roll?

Which cards should you put down when it is your opponent's turn to roll?

Birthday Bars

Some people think that you can tell a lot about others if you know when they were born. Try this activity to make and compare bar graphs of birthdays.

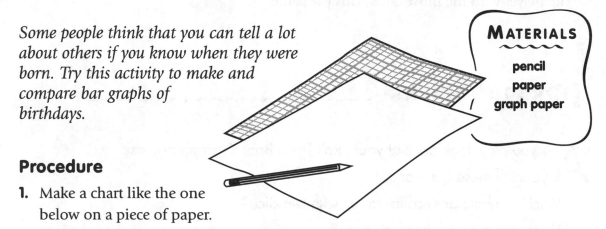

MATERIALS

pencil
paper
graph paper

Procedure

1. Make a chart like the one below on a piece of paper.

Name	Birthday	Zodiac Sign

2. List family members and friends in column 1 of your chart.

3. Add each person's birthday to the chart in column 2.

4. Figure out each person's zodiac sign using the list below. Enter each person's zodiac sign in the far right column of the chart. The 12 signs of the zodiac are

    Aries: March 21–April 19

    Taurus: April 20–May 20

    Gemini: May 21–June 20

    Cancer: June 21–July 22

    Leo: July 23–August 22

    Virgo: August 23–September 22

    Libra: September 23–October 22

    Scorpio: October 23–November 21

    Sagittarius: November 22–December 21

    Capricorn: December 22–January 19

    Aquarius: January 20–February 18

    Pisces: February 19–March 20

5. Make a bar graph that represents the number of your family and friends who were born under each zodiac sign. Put the zodiac signs on the horizontal axis and the numbers 0 to 5 on the vertical axis. Give this graph a title, such as "Zodiac Bars."

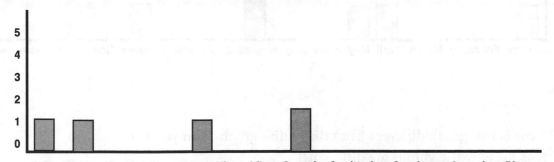

Zodiac Bars

6. Make a new chart that looks like the one on this page. Put the names of the months in the left-hand column and the total number of people who have a birthday in that month in the right-hand column.

7. Graph the birthdays. Put the names of the months on the horizontal axis and the numbers 0 to 5 on the vertical axis. Make a bar graph that shows the number of your friends and family with a birthday in each month. Give your graph a title, such as "Birthday Bars."

Month	Number of Persons with Birthday in the Month
January	
February	
March	
April	
May	
June	
July	
August	
September	
October	
November	
December	

Birthday Bars

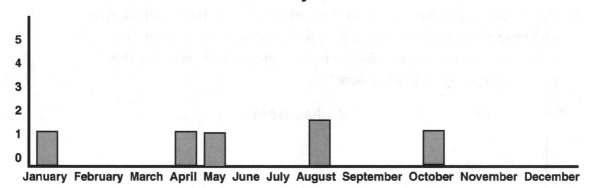

8. How is this graph different from the zodiac graph? Can you think of two reasons why the graphs are different?

The signs of the Chinese zodiac are Rat, Ox, Tiger, Rabbit, Dragon, Snake, Horse, Sheep, Monkey, Rooster, Dog, and Pig. You can figure out a person's Chinese horoscope if you know the year in which he or she was born (see the chart below).

Chinese Horoscope Sign	Year of Birth
Rat	1948, 1960, 1972, 1984, 1996
Ox	1949, 1961, 1973, 1985, 1997
Tiger	1950, 1962, 1974, 1986, 1998
Rabbit	1951, 1963, 1975, 1987, 1999
Dragon	1940, 1952, 1964, 1976, 1988, 2000
Snake	1941, 1953, 1965, 1977, 1989, 2001
Horse	1942, 1954, 1966, 1978, 1990, 2002
Sheep	1943, 1955, 1967, 1979, 1991, 2003
Monkey	1944, 1956, 1968, 1980, 1992, 2004
Rooster	1945, 1957, 1969, 1981, 1993, 2005
Dog	1946, 1958, 1970, 1982, 1994
Pig	1947, 1959, 1971, 1983, 1995

Now figure out how many members of your family and friends fall under each sign of the Chinese horoscope. Graph the results. Does this graph look anything like the other two graphs? Why or why not?

Bouncing Balls

Experiment with bouncing different-size balls and make a double bar graph to compare the two results.

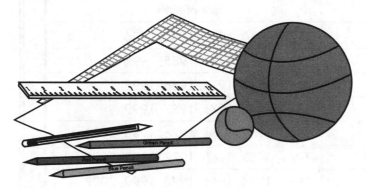

Procedure

1. Copy the chart below on a piece of paper.

Height of Drop	Small Ball Bounces	Large Ball Bounces
1 foot		
3 feet		
5 feet		

2. Find a hard surface and measure 1 foot from the ground. Drop the small ball from 1 foot high and count the number of times it bounces before stopping. Enter the result in the chart.

3. Next, drop the large ball from 1 foot high. Count the number of times it bounces. Enter the result in the chart.

4. Drop each ball from a height of 3 feet. How many times did each ball bounce? Enter the results in the chart.

5. Drop each ball from a height of 5 feet. How many times did each ball bounce? Enter the results in the chart.

6. Graph the results. Use the following graph as a guide. Put the height of the drop and the ball size on the horizontal axis. Put the number of bounces on the vertical axis.

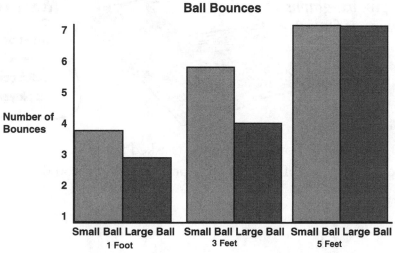

Ball Bounces

7. Use one color to fill in the bars that represent the small ball, and use another color to fill in the bars that represent the large ball.

8. Does ball size affect the number of bounces? Does the height from which the ball is dropped affect the number of bounces?

BRAIN Stretcher

Find a medium-size ball, and drop it from 1, 3, and 5 feet. Count the number of bounces at each height. Construct a new bar graph that compares all three balls. What can you conclude about ball size and the number of bounces? What other factors may affect the ball bouncing?

Pet Survey

Learn how to interpret bar graphs while playing a game of finding fact cards that match that data in a group.

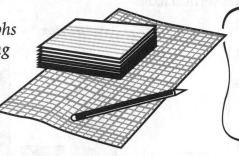

MATERIALS

graph paper
pencil
index cards
2 players

Game Preparation

1. A classroom of 20 students (10 boys and 10 girls) is asked the following question: If you could have one of the following pets, which pet would you pick?

   dog   parakeet   ferret
   cat   fish

   The results of the survey are represented in the bar graph below.

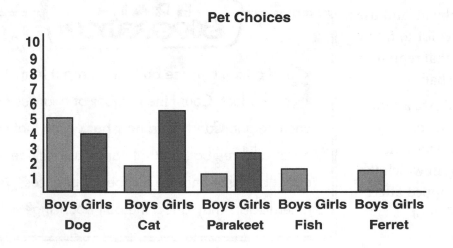

Pet Choices

2. Copy each of the following statements on a separate index card:

The boys' favorite pet was a dog.

More girls than boys picked cats.

Fish were the most popular pets.

Dogs were the most popular pets.

Cats were the most popular pets.

The girls' favorite pet was a dog.

More boys than girls picked cats.

Ferrets were the most popular pets.

Parakeets were the most popular pets.

Dogs were picked least often.

Cats were picked least often.

Parakeets were picked least often.

Ferrets were picked more often than fish.

Girls and boys picked one pet equally.

There was at least one pet that no one picked.

There was at least one pet that no girls picked.

There was at least one pet that no boys picked.

Add some cards of your own.

Game Rules

1. Shuffle the index cards and place them facedown in the center of the table.

2. Players take turns drawing cards from the pile. If the statement on the card is true according to the graph the player drew, the player gets to keep the card. If the card is false, the player puts it in the discard pile in the center of the table.

3. After the players go through the entire stack of cards, the player who kept the most cards wins the game.

BRAIN Stretcher

Survey 20 members of your family and friends with the same question. Graph the results. Now ask the same 20 people which pet they would *not* want to have:

dog

cat

parakeet

fish

ferret

Graph the results. Are the two graphs related? If so, how?

~ IV ~
PIE CHARTS

A pie chart looks like a picture of a pie cut into slices. A pie chart can have as few as two slices or it can have many slices. The slices are usually different sizes and colors. Pie charts are most often used to compare percentages. The entire pie is equal to 100%, and the size of each pie slice corresponds to a percentage amount.

In this part, you will use pie charts to track the dessert consumption of your family members, the chance of tossing heads or tails on a coin, the types of shoes you own, tic-tac-toe competitions, and the favorite colors of family and friends. Grab a compass or a saucer, and start making pie charts!

Just Desserts

Learn to make simple pie charts using desserts.

MATERIALS

pencil
paper
compass or
saucer
ruler
colored pencils
8 cookies,
crackers, or
potato chips
plate for cookies

Procedure

1. Draw a circle on a piece of paper by using a compass or tracing around a saucer.

2. Use the ruler to draw a line across the center of the circle. Draw a second line to cut the circle into 4 equal pieces.

3. Draw two more lines so that you divide the circle into a total of 8 equal pieces.

4. Have each member of your family select a colored pencil.

5. Place the 8 cookies on a plate in the center of the table.

6. Tell the members of your family to eat the cookies at their normal rate. Each time anyone (including yourself) takes a cookie, he or she must

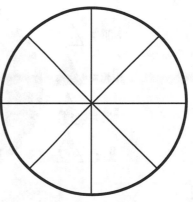

color in a slice of the pie chart with his or her colored pencil. When the cookies are gone, the pie chart will be all colored in and you will be able to see how many cookies each person ate.

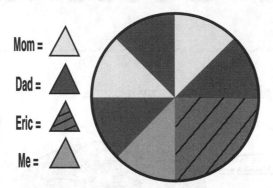

7. Now recopy the chart you drew, but this time put all the same pie wedges of the same color together. Alongside the chart, have everyone write their name and shade a pie slice with their colored pencil. This will serve as the key for the chart. Anyone looking at the chart can tell right away how many cookies each person ate. Write a title for the chart at the top of the page.

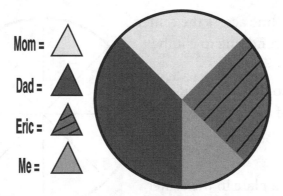

8. On another day, draw a circle and divide it into 16 pieces. Place 16 cookies on a plate. Each time a person eats a cookie, he or she should color in one slice of the circle.

9. Recopy the chart so that all the slices of pie of the same color are together. Add a key and give it a title.

10. Compare the pie charts with the one you drew in step 7. How similar are they? Who ate the most cookies each day? What percentage of the cookies did each person eat each day?

BRAIN Stretcher

The Jones family loves to share a plate of cookies after dinner. One night, a plate of 30 cookies is put out on the table. Mr. Jones eats 6 cookies, Mrs. Jones eats 4 cookies, Sarah Jones eats 3 cookies, and Tom Jones eats 2 cookies. What percent of all the cookies did Mr. Jones eat? If Mr. Jones eats the same percentage of the remaining cookies, how many cookies will he eat?

Flipping Coins

Learn about probability by tossing coins and graphing the results in a pie chart.

Procedure

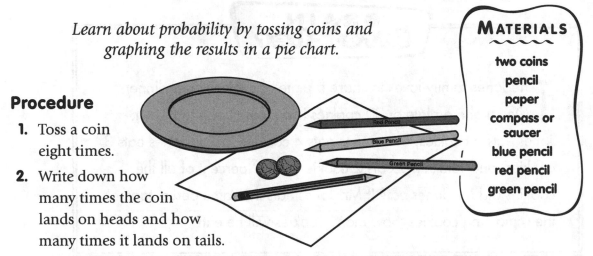

1. Toss a coin eight times.

2. Write down how many times the coin lands on heads and how many times it lands on tails.

3. Draw a circle by using a compass or by tracing around a saucer. Divide the circle into eight equal sections. (First divide it in half, then in half again. Now you have four sections. Divide each of these four sections into two sections to make eight sections.)

4. Shade one section blue for each time the coin lands on heads. Shade one section red for each time the coin lands on tails. The result is a pie chart.

5. What percentage of the tosses were red? What percentage of the tosses were blue?

6. At the top of the chart, write the title "Single-Coin Toss." Below the chart, write the key:

    Blue = Heads

    Red = Tails

7. Now draw a second circle and divide it into eight sections.

8. Toss *two* coins eight times.

9. Shade one section blue each time you toss two heads. Shade one section red each time you toss two tails. Shade one section green each time you roll one head and one tail.

10. At the top of the chart, write the title "Two-Coin Toss." Below the chart, write the key:

Blue = Two heads

Red = Two tails

Green = One head and one tail

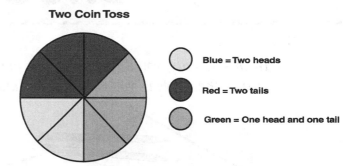

Two Coin Toss

Blue = Two heads

Red = Two tails

Green = One head and one tail

11. When you toss a single coin in the air, the chance of it landing on heads is one out of two, or one-half. Were half of all your coin tosses heads? Why or why not? When you toss two coins in the air, the chance of tossing two heads is one-fourth, the chance of tossing two tails is one-fourth, and the chance of tossing one head and one tail is one-half. Did your pie chart show this?

BRAIN Stretcher

Toss three coins 16 times. How many different possible outcomes are there? Make a pie chart of the results.

13 Shoes... Shoes... Shoes

In this activity, you'll learn to make pie charts using the shoes in your closet as a database.

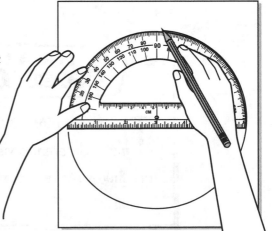

MATERIALS

paper
protractor
pencil
shoes
colored pencils

Procedure

1. Using a protractor, draw two circles on a sheet of paper.

2. Count how many pairs of shoes you have in your closet.

3. Divide each circle into equal sections to match the number of pairs of shoes you have. Each section will now represent one pair of shoes. In order to divide the circles into equal sections, divide 360

(the number of degrees in an entire circle) by the number of pairs of shoes you have. Now you know how many degrees each slice of your pies should be.

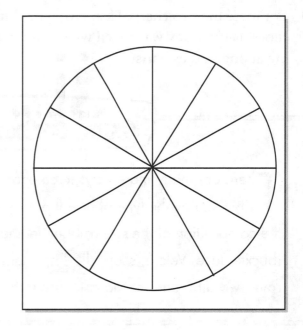

4. Now place the protractor inside each circle and mark off sections that are the same number of degrees as you calculated. Example: If you have 12 pairs of shoes, then divide 360 by 12. The answer is 30. Divide the circle into twelve 30-degree sections.

5. Now sort your shoes by type. Place them in the following groups:

    boots

    sneakers

    dress shoes

    sandals

    slippers

    other

6. Shade one slice of one of the pies for each pair of shoes you have. Shade all the boots one color, all the sneakers a second color, all the dress shoes a third color, all the sandals a fourth color, all the slippers a fifth color, and all of the "other" shoes a sixth color. Make a key so that people who look at your chart can understand the types of shoes you have.

7. Now sort the shoes by their actual color. For example, separate your black shoes, white shoes, blue shoes, and so on. Use the colored pencils to color one slice of the chart the color of each pair of the shoes.

8. Compare the two charts. Each gives you different information about your shoes. Is there any way to tell what color your dress shoes are from looking at one of the charts?

BRAIN Stretcher

There are many more ways to categorize shoes. You could classify them by the type of heel that they have (high, medium, flat), the composition of the sole (rubber, leather), or how they fasten (buckle, lace, Velcro, snap, slip-on). Make a pie chart that incorporates two different ways to categorize shoes.

Tic-Tac-Toed

Play tic-tac-toe with two friends and make a pie chart of the results.

> **MATERIALS**
> paper
> pencil
> calculator
> protractor
> colored pencils
> 3 players

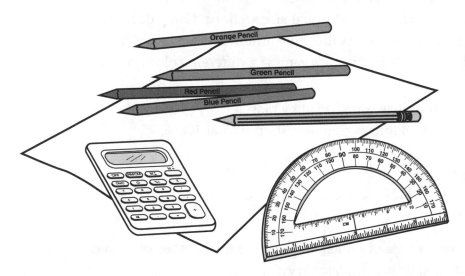

Game Rules

1. Using pencil and paper, the three players take turns playing tic-tac-toe against one another. First player 1 plays player 2, next player 2 plays player 3, and finally player 3 plays player 1. All three of these games equal one round.

2. Players keep track of who wins each game in a chart like this one:

Name of Player	Number of Games Won
Player 1	
Player 2	
Player 3	
"Cat's Game" (Tie Game)	

3. After five rounds, graph the results in a pie chart. If you played five rounds of tic-tac-toe, you played 15 games. To graph the results, use a protractor to draw a circle and divide it into 15 equal-size sections. Using different-colored pencils, each player shades the same number of sections as the number of games won. Shade the "cat's games" a different color from the ones already used.

4. What percentage of the circle was shaded by player 1? By player 2? By player 3? By the "cat"? All four percentages should total 100%.

Tips and Tricks

To compute the percentage of games won, divide the number of games won by 15 and multiply the result by 100.

Color Feud

Learn how to interpret a pie chart while investigating people's favorite colors.

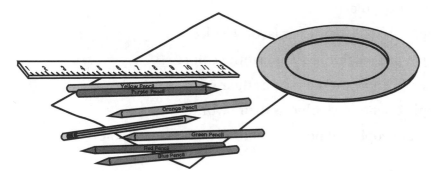

MATERIALS

paper

pencil

compass or saucer

colored pencils

ruler

2 players

Procedure

1. Each player draws two circles using a compass or saucer and divides each circle into 16 sections.

2. Each player colors the sections of one of their circles with the following six colors according to how many people they think will pick each color out of 16 people surveyed:

blue

red

green

yellow

purple

orange

All 16 sections should be colored.

3. Once players finish filling in their circle, they survey 16 people and ask each of them, "Which of the following six colors is your favorite: blue, red, green, yellow, purple, or orange?" For each response to the survey, a section is filled in with the appropriate color in each player's second circle.

4. When all the sections of the second circle are shaded, players compare the results of the survey with their predictions.

5. Look at your survey and answer the following questions:

Which color is most popular?

Which color is least popular?

How many people picked red as their favorite color?

How many people picked blue as their favorite color?

What percentage of people picked blue as their favorite color?

How many people did not pick blue as their favorite color?

What percentage of people did not pick blue as their favorite color?

V

LINE GRAPHS

L ine graphs are used to track progress over time. They are formed by connecting a series of points with a line. The horizontal axis of a line graph usually lists units of time, such as hours, days, months, and so on. The vertical axis is usually a measurement or score.

In this part, you will learn to draw and interpret line graphs while growing grass, hitting a ball, charting the progress of a stock, computing calories of foods, tracking temperatures in different cities, and graphing different shapes. Practice making line graphs while learning a lot of interesting things.

Grassy Lines

Grow some grass and use the data to make a line graph.

MATERIALS

small pebbles
large plastic cup
potting soil
grass seed
water
sunny spot
paper
pencil
ruler
graph paper

Procedure

1. Place an inch of pebbles in the bottom of a plastic cup. Put soil in the cup until it is about 1 inch from the top. Sprinkle grass seed on top of the soil. Put a half-inch of soil on top of the grass seed. Water the grass daily and keep the cup in a sunny spot.

2. On a piece of paper, make a chart like the one below to track the height of the grass. Start with day 0, which is the day you planted your grass

Day	Height of Grass, in Inches
0	
1	
2	
3	
4	
5	
6	
7	
8	
9	
10	
11	
12	
13	
14	

seed. Every day record the height of your grass in inches. Measure the height of the tallest strand of grass. If there is not a single strand of grass poking through the dirt, then put 0 in column 2.

3. Now make a line graph of your result on the graph paper. Call your graph "Grass Growth." Along the horizontal axis, place the numbers 0 to 14 to represent the days you measured the growth of the grass. Label the vertical axis from 0 to 8 inches. This represents the height of your grass. Use this graph as a guide.

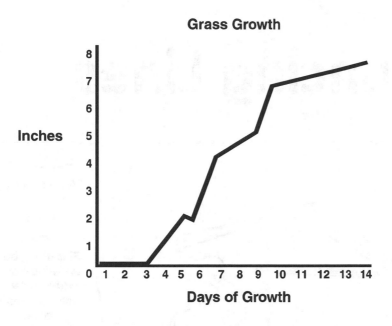

Grass Growth

Inches

Days of Growth

4. Look at your graph and answer the following questions:

How long did it take for the grass to break through the surface of the soil?

During which day did the grass grow the most?

What was the average daily growth of the grass?

BRAIN Stretcher

Plant more seeds in a second cup. Make a three-column chart to record your measurements of both the length of the grass and the length of the roots. Graph both sets of measurements on the same set of axes using two different-colored pencils. Which started to grow sooner; which grew faster; and which grew longer, the grass or its roots?

Bouncing Lines

Practice hitting a ball and learn to graph your improvement at a skill over time.

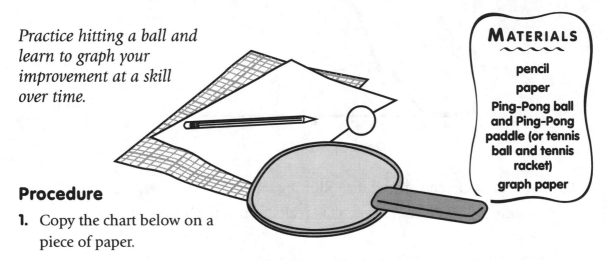

MATERIALS

pencil

paper

Ping-Pong ball and Ping-Pong paddle (or tennis ball and tennis racket)

graph paper

Procedure

1. Copy the chart below on a piece of paper.

Trial	Number of Taps
1	
2	
3	
4	
5	
6	
7	
8	
9	
10	

2. Pick up the Ping-Pong paddle and hit the Ping-Pong ball in the air. How many times in a row did you tap the ball in the air? Enter the results in the "Number of Taps" column on the row marked Trial 1 on the chart.

3. Try a second time and see how many times you can tap the ball in the air. See if you can improve your score. Enter the results in the row marked Trial 2 of the chart.

4. Try eight more times to see if you get better with practice. What was the most times you could tap the ball in the air?

5. Use the data from the chart to construct a line graph. On the horizontal axis, write the numbers 1 to 10. On the vertical axis, write numbers to represent the number of taps.

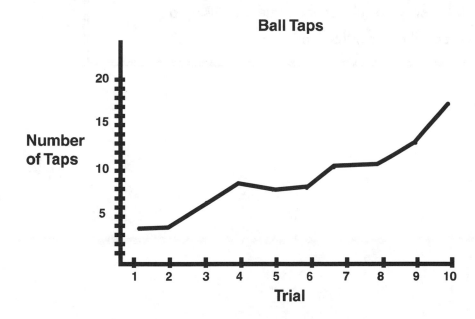

6. Place a small mark above the number 1 on the horizontal axis at the number of successful taps from the first trial. Enter the data in the graph by making a mark above each trial number that is level with the number of taps you did in that trial. Connect all the marks to make a line.

7. One benefit of using a line graph is that it makes it easy to track trends over time. Did your ball tapping increase, stay the same, or decrease over time?

BRAIN Stretcher

Tap the ball with one side of the paddle (or racket), then turn your wrist and tap the ball with the other side. How many times in a row can you tap the ball when you alternate sides? Try 10 different times and graph your results. Ask a friend to do the same thing and graph his or her results on the same axes using a different-colored pencil to draw the line.

Stock Market

Try your hand at picking the best stocks, then graph their results.

MATERIALS

paper
pencil
daily newspaper
or Internet
access
graph paper
colored pencils

Procedure

1. Copy the chart below on a piece of paper.

Day	Price of Stock 1	Price of Stock 2	Price of Stock 3	Price of Stock 4
Week 1—Monday				
Week 1—Tuesday				
Week 1—Wednesday				
Week 1—Thursday				
Week 1—Friday				
Week 2—Monday				
Week 2—Tuesday				
Week 2—Wednesday				
Week 2—Thursday				
Week 2—Friday				

2. Select four stocks to watch over the next two weeks. Here are some possibilities: Coco-Cola (stock symbol: KO), Nike (stock symbol: NKE), Walt Disney (stock symbol: DIS), Dell Computer (stock symbol: DELL), McDonald's (stock symbol: MCD). Look up the stock price at the end of each day by looking up the stock symbol on a stock table in the newspaper or on the Internet.

3. Find the prices for the stocks you picked every day for two weeks and enter the results in the chart.

4. Make a line graph of the results. Draw the line for each stock in a different color. How did your stocks do over the two-week period? Which stock went up the most? Which went down the most?

BRAIN Stretcher

If you bought 100 shares of each stock on Monday of week 1, how much money would you have earned or lost at the end of week 2?

Watching Your Weight

Use a double-line graph to see the calories and fat that you consume in a typical week.

19

MATERIALS

paper
pencil
book that lists
calories and
grams of fat for
various foods
graph paper
colored pencils

Procedure

1. Make a chart like the one below for each day of the week.

Day 1 Food Items	Calories	Grams of Fat
Totals for Day 1		

2. At the end of each day, enter all of the food items you ate in column 1 of the chart.

3. Look up the calories and the grams of fat in everything that you ate, and enter them in columns 2 and 3 of the chart.

4. Write the totals at the bottom of the chart.

5. Copy a chart like the one below on a piece of paper.

Days of Week	Calories	Grams of Fat	Calories from Fat
1			
2			
3			
4			
5			
6			
7			
Total			

6. Enter your daily totals in this chart.

7. Now create a graph that will show both the calories and grams of fat you ate on each day of the week on the same set of axes. On the top of the sheet of graph paper, write the title of the graph: "Calorie and Fat Consumption for One Week." On the horizontal axis, write the numbers to represent the days of the week. Number the left vertical axis from 0 to 3,000 in intervals of 500. Label this axis "Calories." Number the right vertical axis from 0 to 30 in intervals of 2. Label this axis "Grams of Fat."

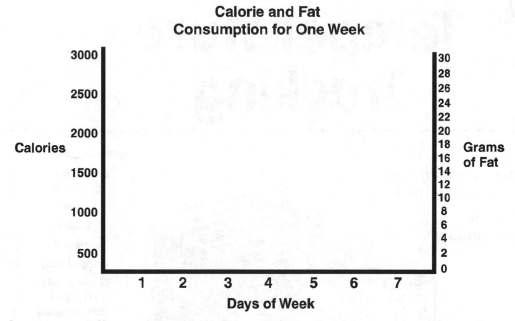

Calorie and Fat Consumption for One Week

Calories: 3000, 2500, 2000, 1500, 1000, 500

Grams of Fat: 30, 28, 26, 24, 22, 20, 18, 16, 14, 12, 10, 8, 6, 4, 2, 0

Days of Week: 1 2 3 4 5 6 7

8. Using a different-colored pencil to make each line, enter your fat and calorie data on the graph. Do you see a relationship between the two lines?

20

Temperature Tracking

Learn to graph three different sets of data on a single line graph as you find out about weather in some U.S. cities.

MATERIALS

paper

scissors

pencil

paper bag

10 consecutive days of newspapers or Internet access

graph paper

2 or more players

Game Preparation

Cut a single sheet of paper into eight small sheets of paper. Write each of the following names of cities on a small sheet of paper: Chicago, New York, Fairbanks, Los Angeles, Miami, Honolulu, Dallas, and Seattle. Fold each of the small sheets of paper and place them in a paper bag.

Game Rules

1. Each player picks a city out of the bag.

2. Players use the newspapers or the Internet to find the high temperature every day for 10 days in the cities they selected.

3. Each player graphs the high temperatures from his or her city. The horizontal axis of the graph will be the days, numbered from 1 to 10, and the vertical axis will be the temperature, from 0 to 100 degrees Fahrenheit. After all the temperatures are graphed, players will be awarded points for the following questions. Give yourself 1 point if your city . . .

   had the highest high temperature

   had the lowest high temperature

   had the greatest range of high temperatures. (To figure it out, find the highest high temperature for each city over the 10-day period and subtract from it the lowest high temperature over that same period for that same city. The city with the greatest difference had the greatest range of temperature.)

   had the same high temperature 2 days in a row

   had high temperatures above 75 degrees

   had high temperatures below 30 degrees

   had 3 days of high temperatures between 30 and 50 degrees

4. The player with the most points wins.

Graphy Diagrams

Play a game where you create graphs that follow a particular shape.

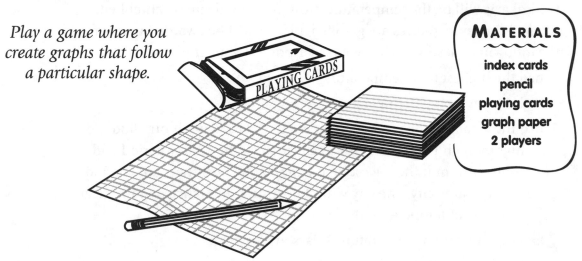

MATERIALS

index cards
pencil
playing cards
graph paper
2 players

Game Preparation

1. Copy each of the following shapes on an index card:

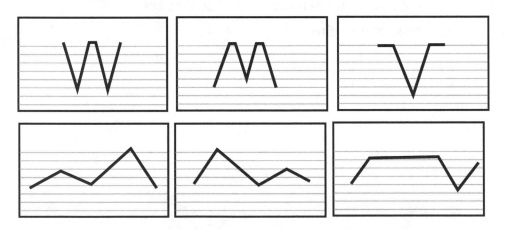

2. Remove all of the face cards from the deck of playing cards.

Game Rules

1. Each player selects one of the six shapes to copy.

2. Deal each player five cards. Place the remaining cards facedown in the center of the table. The numbers on the cards represent points on a graph.

3. Players try to use the numbers on their five cards in any order to make a line graph that is the same shape as the one on the index card they selected. Use graph paper to draw the graph. On the horizontal axis of the graph, write the numbers 1 to 5 to represent the five cards. On the vertical axis, write the numbers 1 to 10 to represent the numbers on the cards.

4. If neither player can copy his or her drawing using his or her original five cards, they take turns drawing a playing card from the stack in the center of the table. After a player draws a card, he or she must discard one. Discarded cards should be placed faceup in the center of the table. Players should have five cards in their hands at all times.

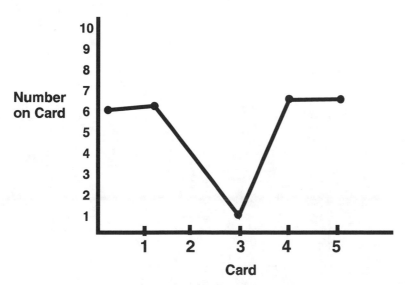

5. The first player to make a copy of his or her drawing wins the game.

VI MAP CHARTS

Charts made of maps are used to answer the question "Where?" Where is it raining? Where does a certain animal live? Where is a certain product manufactured? Map charts are easy ways to learn a lot about different parts of the United States and the world.

In this part, you will learn where the members of your family have traveled, where the mail in your house originated, where various items in your house were made, and how to read weather maps.

22

Family Travel

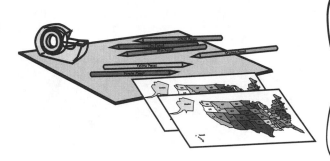

Learn how to construct a map chart.

Procedure

1. Look at a map of the United States. If you have visited a particular state, shade that state red. If you have not visited a particular state, shade it blue.

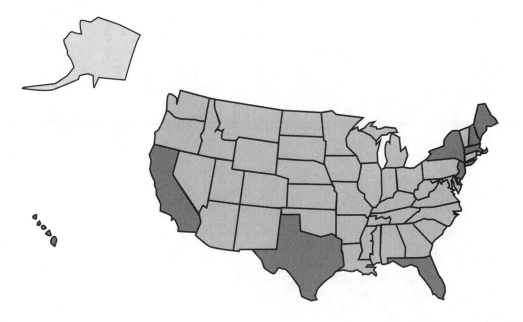

2. Fill out a similar map for each member of your family. Label each person's map with his or her name.

3. On an extra map, color a state purple if any member of your family has visited that state and color it pink if no one has visited it. Label the purple states that all members of your family have visited "Everyone."

4. Tape all the maps onto a single piece of poster board. Title the poster board "Family Travel."

23

Mail Call

Learn to make a map diagram of where your family's mail comes from.

MATERIALS

1 week's worth of mail

photocopy of U.S. map

paper

pencil

colored pencils

Procedure

1. Examine every piece of mail that comes into your house over the next week. Look at the postmark to see which state each piece of mail came from.

2. Make a list of what you find by putting a slash mark beside the name of the state for each piece of mail.

EXAMPLE

Alabama: ///

Delaware: /

New York: ////

3. On the U.S. map, color all the states that you got a piece of mail from blue, and color the states that you did not get any mail from red.

4. In the center of each blue state write the number of pieces of mail received from that state.

The postmark, which is stamped on a letter by the post office, not only tells where a letter was mailed but also the time and date it was mailed.

For a more complex chart, include not only where each piece of mail came from but also how long it took for that piece of mail to get to your house.

Make a list of the states the mail came from, but instead of putting a slash mark for each piece of mail that came into your house, put the number of days it took for the mail to get to you.

Example

California: 3, 5, 2, 2

Ohio: 1, 2, 1

Now average the number of days for each state.

California = 12/4 = 3

Ohio = 4/3 = 1.33

On a U.S. map, assign a different-colored pencil for each number of days and color in each state that you received mail from according to the average number of days it took the mail to come from that state. For example, your color key could be as follows:

1 day = pink

2 days = orange

3 days = yellow

4 days = red

5 days = blue

6 days = green

7 days = purple

Be sure to draw your color key on the map.

What can you conclude about postal delivery by looking at your completed map? Does the mail coming from states that are farthest from your home take the longest to reach you?

Around the World

Learn where the items in your house were made and how to make a world graph.

MATERIALS

paper
pencil
various household
items (see chart)
scissors
colored pencils
glue
map of the world

Procedure

1. Copy the following chart on a piece of paper.

Item	Where It was Made
Dishes	
Spaghetti	
Cereal	
Dishes	
Sweater	
Blue Jeans	
Sneakers	
Pots and Pans	
Television	
Telephone	
Book	
CD Player	
Toaster	

2. Find the items in your house listed on the chart and try to figure out where each was manufactured.

3. Put the country of origin next to each item in the chart. There are a few blank spaces at the end of the chart for you to add items of your choice.

4. Draw small pictures of the items in the list or cut out pictures of the items from ads in a newspaper or magazine.

5. Glue each picture you drew or cut out on the map of the world on the country where the item was manufactured.

BRAIN Stretcher

Make a list of 50 items in your house and identify where each item was manufactured. Group the items by the continent in which they were manufactured. There are seven continents:

North America

South America

Europe

Asia

Africa

Australia

Antarctica

How many items were made on each continent? Make a bar graph to show your results.

Weather Bingo

Learn to interpret a weather map.

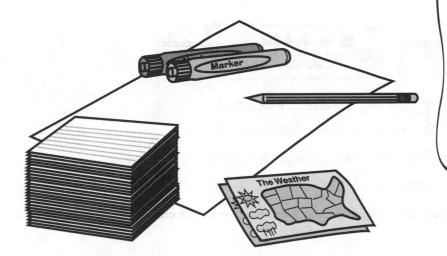

MATERIALS

25 index cards
pencil
paper
several weather
maps cut out
from old
newspapers
2 markers
2 or more players

Game Preparation

Write each of the following phrases on an index card:

temperature in Florida over 90 degrees

snow in New England

below 0 degrees Fahrenheit anywhere in the United States

snow in Texas

rain in Hawaii

Make up other weather phrases like these for the other 20 index cards.

Game Rules

1. Shuffle the index cards and place them facedown in the center of the table.

2. Each player chooses a weather map.

3. The index cards are turned over one at a time. Players use markers to circle the described weather on their map if they have it.

4. The first player to circle five different weather items wins the game.

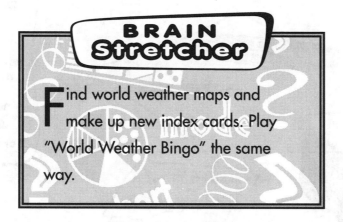

BRAIN Stretcher

Find world weather maps and make up new index cards. Play "World Weather Bingo" the same way.

VII

ALL ABOUT GRAPHS AND CHARTS

Now that you know how to make pictographs, bar graphs, line graphs, pie charts, and map charts, it's time to put your knowledge to the test. Try these four fun activities and see what you've learned!

Graphing Comparisons

Learn to compare different kinds of graphs.

MATERIALS

newspaper
scissors
pencil
paper
calculator
graph paper
colored pencils
poster board
glue

Procedure

1. Copy the chart below on a piece of paper.

Vowel	Number of Occurrences	Percentage of Occurrences
A		
E		
I		
O		
U		
Total		100%

2. Cut out two paragraphs from the newspaper.

3. Circle all the vowels (a, e, i, o, u) in the paragraphs you cut out.

4. Count the number of a's, e's, i's, o's, and u's. What is the total number of vowels in the two paragraphs? Fill in the chart with the results.

5. Compute the percentage of each vowel's occurrence by dividing the number of each vowel by the total number of vowels. Multiply the result by 100. Use your calculator for help. Enter the percentage in the chart.

6. Draw a bar graph of your findings. Put the names of the vowels on the horizontal axis. Put the number of times the vowel occurred on the vertical axis. Label your graph. Write "Vowels" under the horizontal axis and "Occurrences" alongside the vertical axis. Color each bar a different color.

7. Draw a line graph of your findings. Put the vowels on the horizontal axis. Put the number of times the vowel occurred on the vertical axis. Label the horizontal and vertical axes.

8. Draw a pictograph of the results. Put the vowels on the horizontal axis. Make a scale. For example, let each letter represent five occurrences of a certain vowel. So, if there are 30 letter a's in the passage you selected, line up 6 letter a's. Label your pictograph with the scale.

9. Draw a pie chart of the results. Use the percentages you computed to make your pie chart. Fill in each section of the pie chart with a different color. Use a key to show which color represents which vowel.

10. Take all four graphs and charts and glue them on a large piece of poster board. Give the poster board the title "Vowel Frequency" or choose your own title.

11. Show your poster with your graphs and charts on it to other family members or friends. Ask them which graph or chart is easiest to read. What do you think are the advantages and disadvantages of each type of chart?

Scavenger Hunt

Explore the ways that graphs are used in newspapers.

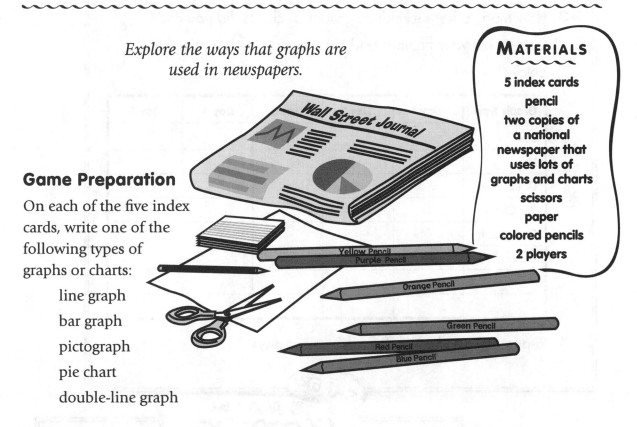

MATERIALS

5 index cards

pencil

two copies of a national newspaper that uses lots of graphs and charts

scissors

paper

colored pencils

2 players

Game Preparation

On each of the five index cards, write one of the following types of graphs or charts:

> line graph
>
> bar graph
>
> pictograph
>
> pie chart
>
> double-line graph

Game Rules

1. Turn over the cards and shuffle them. Deal each player two cards.

2. Each player takes a copy of the newspaper and looks for the types of graphs or charts that match his or her cards. Players cut out as many graphs or charts of the right type as they find. The player who finds the most graphs or charts that match his or her cards wins the game.

BRAIN Stretcher

1. Get another copy of the same newspaper and cut out all the graphs and charts.

2. Sort all the graphs by type.

3. How many different kinds of graphs or charts did you find? Categorize your findings and enter them in a chart like the one below.

Graph Type	Day 1	Day 2	Day 3	Day 4	Day 5
Bar					
Line					
Double Line					
Pie Chart					
Pictograph					
Other					

4. Repeat steps 1 through 3 for four more days.

SUPER BRAIN Stretcher

Display the results from each day in the Brain Stretcher activity above as a pie chart. Indicate each different type of graph with a different color.

Who Done It?

Learn to interpret graphs without the data.

MATERIALS

graph paper
pencil
paper
several players

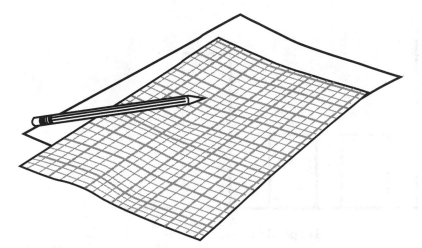

Procedure

1. Below are three graphs. Each graph represents a set of data. Match each graph to one of the stories below. Answers are on page 85.

Graph 1

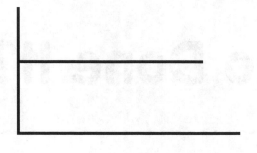

Graph 2

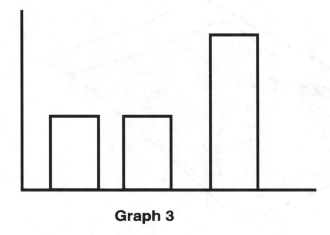

Graph 3

Stories:

> **Story A.** Jodi is an excellent student. She scored the same on five spelling tests in a row.

> **Story B.** Linda wears blue jeans to school half of the time. Next often, she wears shorts, and once in a while she wears a skirt.

> **Story C.** All three children in a family counted the number of glasses of orange juice that each drank per week. Two of the children drank the same amount, while the third drank twice as much.

2. Now that you know how to match a story to a graph, it is time to create your own graphs and stories. Draw one bar graph, one line graph, and one pie chart.

3. Create short stories that match each of your graphs.

Now that you know how to match a graph to a story, it is time to play "Who Done It." Player 1 draws a mystery graph on a sheet of paper. The horizontal and vertical axes are not marked. Each player secretly writes a story to match the graph. The stories are passed to the person who drew the graph. He or she reads all the stories aloud and everyone votes on the most creative one and the writer of that story gets 1 point. The next player draws a mystery graph and the rest of the players write stories. When each player has had a turn drawing a mystery graph, the game is over. The player with the most points wins the game.

Answers:

    Story A — graph 2

    Story B — graph 1

    Story C — graph 3

Word Search

Create a word search game using graphing words to help you remember them.

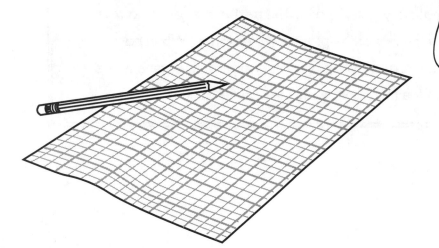

Game Preparation

Both players create a word search using graph paper and a pencil. Put one letter in each box of the graph paper to hide the following 12 words in your word search. The words can be read horizontally, vertically, or diagonally.

> pie chart
> tally
> pictograph
> key
> bar graph

line graph

double-line graph

horizontal

vertical

axes

title

percent

Fill in the empty spaces with random letters.

Game Rules

1. Once both players have finished constructing their word searches, they exchange word searches and solve each other's word search.

2. The first person to find all of the words in the puzzle wins the game.

VIII

STATISTICS

Statistics is used in science, math, education, and business to interpret data. With statistics, you can calculate the average or mean of a set of numbers, find the mode, understand what the range is, compute percentiles, and much more!

In this part you will play some "mean" games, learn to compute your grade-point average (GPA), survey the sleep habits of your family and friends, test the memory of your friends, and more as you learn about different kinds of statistics.

Mean Solitaire

Play the game of solitaire and learn to compute the mean of your scores.

MATERIALS

playing cards or computer with solitaire game
paper
pencil
calculator

Game Rules

1. Play a game of solitaire. When the game is over, count how many cards you were able to place in the piles with the aces (including aces).

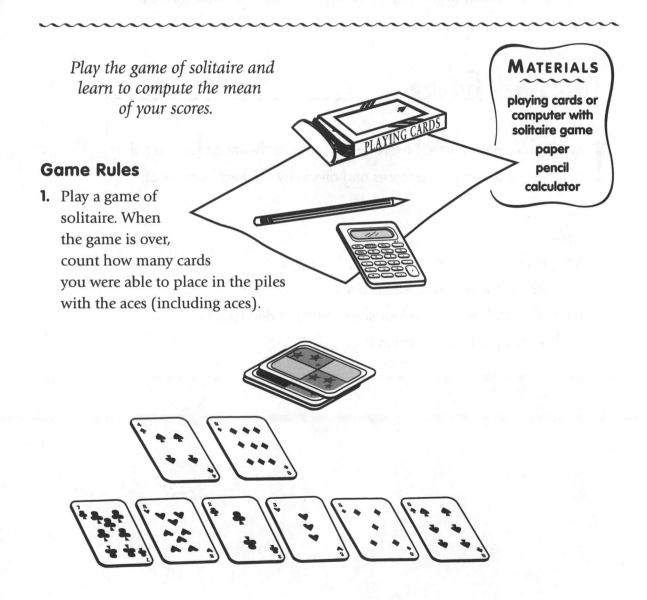

2. Give yourself 1 point for each of the cards placed on the piles with the aces (including aces). Write down the number of points you earned.

3. Play nine more games of solitaire and record the number of points you earned in each of these games.

4. Compute the mean number of cards won. Use the calculator for help.

Tips and Tricks

The mean is the arithmetic average. To compute the mean for a set of numbers, just add all the scores and divide by the total number of scores.

Example

What is the mean of the numbers 3, 5, 7, and 9?

Just add all four scores together: 3 + 5 + 7 + 9 = 24.

Divide the total by 4, since four scores were added together.

24 divided by 4 is 6. The mean is 6.

Matching Means

Play this game to practice computing means. Watch how the mean changes as new scores are added.

MATERIALS

30 index cards
pencil for each player
1 die
calculator
piece of paper for each player
2 to 4 players

Game Preparation

Write each of the following numbers on a separate index card:

0	0	0	0	0
50	50	60	70	70
70	70	80	80	80
80	80	90	90	90
90	100	100	100	100
100	100	100	100	100

Game Rules

1. Shuffle the index cards and deal each player seven cards.

2. Place the remaining cards facedown in the center of the table. Turn over the top card and place it faceup on the table. This is the target mean. Players will try to pick cards from their hand so that their mean matches the target mean.

3. One player rolls one die. The number on the die indicates the number of cards to be selected.

4. Each player selects the same number of cards from his or her hand and places them faceup on the table. Players pick the cards so that their average will match as close to the target mean as possible.

5. Each player's cards are averaged. The player with the average closest to the target mean wins the game.

EXAMPLE

The target mean is 60. The die is 4, so each player places four cards on the table. Player 1 puts 50, 60, 70, and 80 on the table. Player 2 puts 0, 100, 50, and 90 on the table. Each player's cards are averaged. Player 1's average is 50 + 60 + 70 + 80 = 260/4 = 65. Player 2's average is 0 + 100 + 50 + 100 = 250/4 = 62.5. Player 2's target mean is closer to 60. So, player 2 gets 1 point for that round. The first player to get 3 points wins the game.

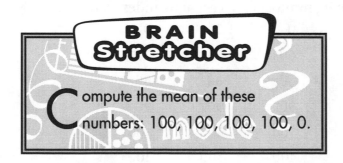

BRAIN Stretcher

Compute the mean of these numbers: 100, 100, 100, 100, 0.

Estimating Means

Guess the mean of a changing set of numbers without computing it.

MATERIALS

24 index cards
pencil
paper
calculator
red and blue
pencils

Game Preparation

Write each of the following numbers on a separate index card:

0	0	10	10
20	20	30	30
30	30	40	40
50	50	60	60
70	70	80	80
90	90	100	100

Game Rules

1. Shuffle the index cards and place them facedown in the center of the table.

2. Copy the chart on the following page on a sheet of paper.

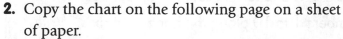

3. Turn over the top card. This is your first score. This is also the mean. Enter the score and the mean in the chart.

4. Turn over the next card in the deck. Add this number to the previous number to get the new score and guess the new mean. Now calculate the new mean. How accurate was your guess? Enter the new score and the new mean in the chart.

Card Number	Score	Mean
1		
2		
3		
4		
5		
6		
7		
8		
9		
10		

5. Turn over the next card. Add this number to the previous two numbers and guess the mean of all three scores. Now calculate the new mean. How accurate was your guess? Enter the new score and the new mean in the chart.

6. Repeat the process of turning over the next card and finding the new mean until a total of 10 cards have been turned over. Fill in the chart with your results.

BRAIN Stretcher

Use a line graph to compare the fluctuations in scores with the fluctuations in the mean. Write the numbers 1 to 10 along the horizontal axis. Write the numbers 0, 10, 20, 30, 40, 50, 60, 70, 80, 90, and 100 along the vertical axis. Graph the 10 scores you selected. Connect the scores with a red line. Then graph the 10 means you calculated and connect the means with a blue pencil. How do the two graphs compare?

GPA

Learn to compute your grade-point average (GPA).
(High schools use GPA to determine class rank.
The student with the highest GPA is called the
valedictorian of the class. The student
with the second highest GPA is
called the salutatorian.
Colleges use a student's
GPA as one factor in
assessing whether a student
will be admitted.)

MATERIALS

paper
pencil
your last report
card
calculator

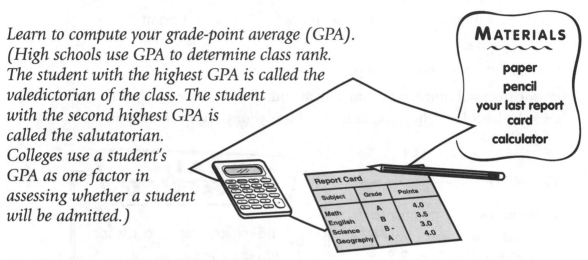

Procedure

1. Copy the chart below on a piece of paper.

Subject	Grade	Points
Total Points		

2. Find your last report card and enter the subjects and the grades in the chart.

3. To figure out the GPA, give each grade the following number of points:

A+ = 4 points	A = 3.7 points	A– = 3.5 points
B+ = 3.3 points	B = 3 points	B– = 2.7 points
C+ = 2.5 points	C = 2 points	C– = 1.7 points
D+ = 1.5 points	D = 1.3 points	D– = 1 point
F = 0 points		

4. Calculate the total number of points you earned.

5. Divide the total number of points by the number of classes you took. Use the calculator for help if you need to. This is your GPA for that report card.

EXAMPLE ～～～～～

If you earned 14 points and you took five classes, your GPA is 14 divided by 5, or 2.8.

BRAIN Stretcher

Find all your report cards for last year. Compute your GPA for each of your report cards. Then find your average GPA for the year.

Tower Tallies

The mode *is defined as the most frequent score in a set of scores. Learn to compute the mode while playing a coin toss game.*

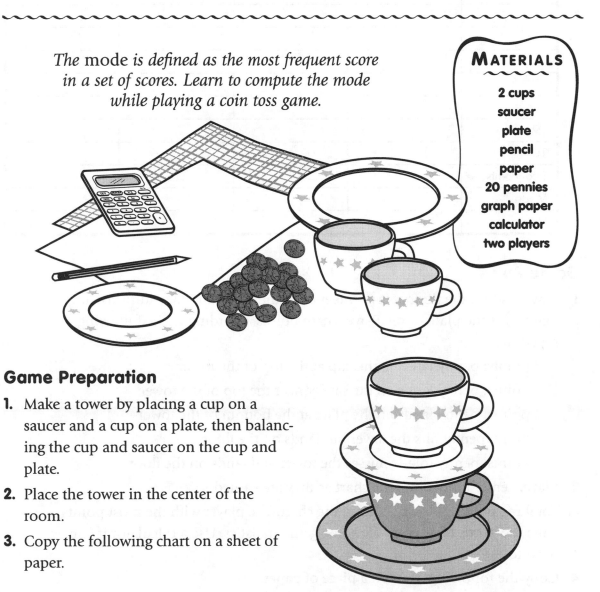

MATERIALS

2 cups
saucer
plate
pencil
paper
20 pennies
graph paper
calculator
two players

Game Preparation

1. Make a tower by placing a cup on a saucer and a cup on a plate, then balancing the cup and saucer on the cup and plate.

2. Place the tower in the center of the room.

3. Copy the following chart on a sheet of paper.

Toss Number	Game 1		Game 2	
	Player 1	Player 2	Player 1	Player 2
1				
2				
3				
4				
5				
6				
7				
8				
9				
10				
Total Points				
Mode				
Mean				

Game Rules

1. Players sit on the floor at least 5 feet from the tower and take turns tossing pennies at the plate tower. Players earn points according to the following schedule:

　　5 points: penny lands in the cup at the top of the tower

　　3 points: penny lands on the saucer near the top of the tower

　　2 points: penny lands on the plate at the bottom of the tower

　　1 point: penny hits the tower but lands on the floor

　　0 points: penny totally misses the tower and lands on the floor

2. Players enter points into the chart as they are earned.

3. Total the points at the bottom of the chart. The player with the most points wins the game. Now compute some game statistics. Use a calculator if you need to.

4. Copy the following chart on a piece of paper.

Score	Game 1		Game 2	
	Player 1	Player 2	Player 1	Player 2
5 points				
3 points				
2 points				
1 point				
0 points				

5. Count how many times each player earned 5 points. Now count how many times each player earned 3, 2, 1, and 0 points. Enter the tallies in the chart.

6. Which score has the highest frequency? This is the mode. What is the mode for player 1? What is the mode for player 2? If you had the same frequency for two different scores, then your score is *bimodal*. Report both scores.

7. Now compute the mean for each player. The mean is the arithmetic average. Just divide the total points earned by 10 (the number of trials) to compute the mean.

8. On a piece of graph paper, graph your results with the toss numbers on the horizontal axis and the scores on the vertical axis. What can you learn from looking at the graph that you cannot learn from looking at the statistics? What can you learn from looking at the statistics that you cannot learn from looking at the graph?

BRAIN Stretcher

Build a more complex tower out of plates, saucers, cups, and anything else you can find. Assign point values for various parts of your tower. Toss 25 coins and compute your game statistics.

Highest Median

The median is defined as the number where half of the numbers in a set are below it and half of the numbers in the set are above it. For example, in the set 1, 2, 6, 7, 11, the median is 6. Learn how to compute the median by playing this fun card game.

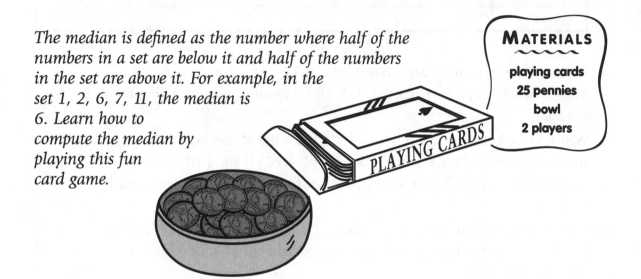

MATERIALS

playing cards
25 pennies
bowl
2 players

Game Preparation

1. Remove the face cards from a deck of playing cards. Shuffle the remaining cards and place them facedown in the center of the table.

2. Place a bowl with the pennies in the center of the table.

Game Rules

1. Players each draw three cards and place them faceup in front of them.

2. Each player puts his or her cards in numerical order from smallest to largest.

3. The center card is the median. The player with the highest median takes a penny from the bowl.

4. Players each draw two cards. Each player places the new cards in order in his or her row and computes a new median. The player with the highest median wins another penny.

5. Play is repeated five times. The player with the most pennies at the end wins the game.

Tips and Tricks

If there is an odd number of scores in a set, the median is the middle score. If there is an even number of scores in a set, the median is the average of the two middlemost scores.

Example

In the set 1, 2, 3, 4, 5 (which has an odd number of terms), the median is simply 3. In the set 1, 2, 3, 4, 5, 6 (which has an even number of terms), the median is the average of 3 and 4, which is 3.5.

BRAIN Stretcher

Play "Highest Median" again. This time players pick only one new card at each new round.

Hit the Target

Learn to compare the mean, mode, and median while playing a card game.

MATERIALS

playing cards
2 dice
paper
pencil
calculator
2 players

Game Preparation

Remove the face cards from the deck of playing cards.

Game Rules

1. Each player rolls the dice. If a player rolls 10, 11, or 12, he or she rolls again. The number rolled is the player's target number.

2. Each player is dealt five cards. The remaining cards are placed facedown in the center of the table.

3. Players calculate the mean, mode, and median of the cards in their hand. Use the calculaor for help. In order to win, the mean, mode, or median must equal a player's target number.

4. Player 1 draws the top card from the center pile and discards a card so that he or she always has five cards. Player 1 computes the mean, mode, and median of the five cards in his or her hand and sees if any of the results are his or her target number.

104

5. Player 2 draws the top card and discards a single card from his or her hand. Player 2 computes the mean, mode, and median of these five cards to determine if any of these results is his or her target number.

6. The player who hits his or her target number wins the round.

7. The first player to win three rounds wins the game.

BRAIN Stretcher

Play "Hit the Target" with all 52 cards in the deck. Let the face cards be wild. A wild card can have any number you want it to from 2 to 12. Deal each player seven cards. Each player rolls the dice to determine his or her target number. The number can be any number from 2 to 12. Players try to make the mean, median, or mode of the cards equal to the number rolled.

Sleep Study

Do a study of sleep habits and learn to report statistical data.

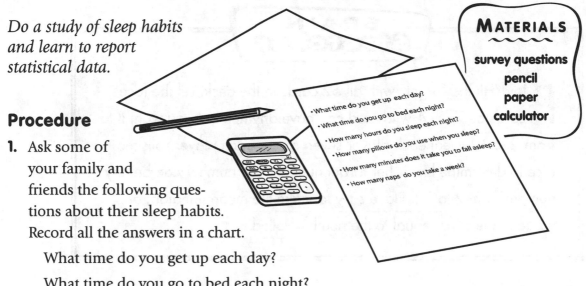

MATERIALS

survey questions
pencil
paper
calculator

Procedure

1. Ask some of your family and friends the following questions about their sleep habits. Record all the answers in a chart.

What time do you get up each day?

What time do you go to bed each night?

How many hours do you sleep each night?

How many pillows do you use when you sleep?

How many minutes does it take you to fall asleep?

How many naps do you take a week?

2. Now compute the mean, the high score, the low score, and the range for each question. Use the calculator for help. The mean is the average score, and the range is the difference between the highest and lowest scores.

EXAMPLE

Seven people were asked the question: "How many naps do you take a week?" Their answers were 3, 0, 1, 1, 2, 0, 7.

The mean or average score is 2.

The high score is 7, and the low score is 0.

The range is the high score (7) minus the low score (0), or 7.

3. Now report the results of the survey. First, write what you did.

EXAMPLE ~~~~~~

Seven people were surveyed regarding their sleep habits. All seven people were asked the following questions:

What time do you get up each day?

What time do you go to bed each night?

How many hours do you sleep each night?

How many pillows do you use when you sleep?

How many minutes does it take you to fall asleep?

How many naps do you take a week?

Then write down the results of your survey.

EXAMPLE ~~~~~~

The average person takes two naps a week. The range was seven, since one person took seven naps a week and two took zero naps a week.

BRAIN Stretcher

Design your own survey about a topic of your choice. Make sure that all of your questions can be answered with a number. Write up the results in a report. Make graphs and charts of some of the results.

Baby Weight

Learn what a normal curve is and how to predict which data follow the normal curve.

MATERIALS

pencil
paper
graph paper

Procedure

1. Copy the chart below on a piece of paper.

Weight Range	Number of Babies in This Weight Range
1 pound–1 pounds 15 ounces	
2 pounds–2 pounds 15 ounces	
3 pounds–3 pounds 15 ounces	
4 pounds–4 pounds 15 ounces	
5 pounds–5 pounds 15 ounces	
6 pounds–6 pounds 15 ounces	
7 pounds–7 pounds 15 ounces	
8 pounds–8 pounds 15 ounces	
9 pounds–9 pounds 15 ounces	
10 pounds–10 pounds 15 ounces	
11 pounds–11 pounds 15 ounces	
12 pounds–12 pounds 15 ounces	
13 pounds–13 pounds 15 ounces	
14 pounds–14 pounds 15 ounces	

2. Survey adults, children, family, and friends. Ask each person how much he or she weighed at birth. The more people you survey, the more accurate the results, so try to survey at least 25 people. Write down all of the answers.

3. Count how many people had birth weights in each of the weight categories in your chart. Put the total number in the right-hand column of the chart.

4. Graph the results as a line graph. Put the numbers that represent each of the weight categories on the horizontal axis. Put the number of people in each category on the vertical axis.

5. What is the shape of the line graph? Certain data sets follow a special shape. This shape is called a *normal curve.* It is highest in the center and it slopes down and tapers off at each end.

A normal curve looks like this:

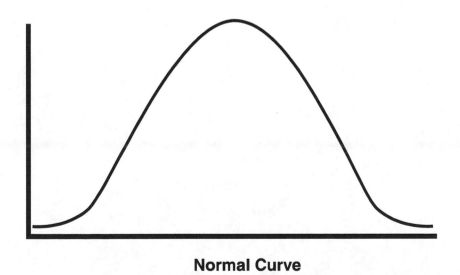

Normal Curve

Does your graph of baby weights look like a normal curve?

Find the heights of 25 adult men and 25 adult women. Graph all 50 people on a single-line graph. Is it a normal curve? Now separate the men from the women into two different graphs. Is either of these graphs a normal curve?

Number Memory

Learn the difference between percents and percentiles while testing your friends' memories.

MATERIALS

10 index cards
paper
pencil
calculator
10 players

Procedure

1. Copy each of the following sets of numbers on a separate index card:

   3, 8, 4

   1, 9, 7, 6

   3, 5, 0, 8, 4

   7, 2, 8, 4, 3, 1

   8, 7, 6, 2, 9, 0, 4

   5, 0, 9, 6, 4, 1, 3, 7

   4, 9, 8, 3, 4, 0, 7, 5, 6

   6, 2, 7, 5, 9, 4, 6, 8, 0, 1

   5, 9, 4, 8, 3, 2, 9, 6, 7, 0, 2

   9, 4, 6, 8, 2, 7, 3, 6, 0, 3, 7, 5

2. Copy the chart below on a piece of paper.

Name	Number Correct	Percentage Correct	Percentile

3. Use the index cards to test the memory of each person, one at a time. Read the numbers on a single card to one person, and ask him or her to repeat the numbers back to you in the order that you read them. Do this for all 10 cards.

4. Write the player's name and the number of cards that he or she repeated correctly in the chart. Test all 10 players.

5. Compute the percentage of cards that each player got correct. Use the calculator if you need to. Divide the number by 10, then multiply the result by 100. For example, if a player got 7 correct, then he or she got 7/10, or 0.7. Multiply this by 100 to get 70%.

6. Now compute each player's percentile. A person's percentile is how he or she scored relative to the group. Enter these results in the chart. To compute a player's percentile, just count the number of players who scored lower than that player. Divide this number by 10, since there are 10 players in the group. Multiply the result by 100. For example, if 5 players scored lower than a particular player, then he or she scored at the 50th percentile.

BRAIN Stretcher

Use 10 more index cards and create 10 new sets of numbers from 2 to 11. Read each card to each player, but ask each player to say the numbers on each card in the reverse order that you read the set. For example, if you read the set 1, 4, 7, then the player should say 7, 4, 1. Compute the percent and percentile for each player. Did players have the same percentage correct in both tests? Did players have the same percentile? Why or why not?

Rank Order

Learn about rank order while enjoying some tasty fruit snacks.

Procedure

1. Copy the chart below on a piece of paper.

Color	Bag 1	Bag 2	Bag 3	Total

2. Open a bag of fruit snacks and sort them by color. What color are most of the fruit snacks in bag 1? Put a 1 next to that color. This color is ranked first in the set. Put a 2 next to the color that is the second most plentiful. Continue until all the colors are ranked. Note: If you have the same number of two colors of fruit snacks, each of those colors gets the same rank. But then you must skip a rank for the next color. For example, if you have the same number of red and green fruit snacks and you have the most of both of them, then they are both ranked 1. The next highest color would have a rank of 3.

3. If you were to eat one fruit snack from each color, does the rank order change?

4. Now open a second bag of fruit snacks and rank them by color. Enter the results in the chart. Are the numbers of fruit snacks of each color the same? Is the ranking the same?

5. Now do the same with a third bag of fruit snacks.

6. Combine all three bags of fruit snacks. Sort and rank each of the colors for the combined bags.

7. How are all of the rankings the same, and how are they different?

BRAIN Stretcher

Compute the average rank for the three bags of fruit snacks. Does this match the combined rank? Why or why not?

Graphs and Statistics Master Certificate

Now that you've mastered all the graphing and statistics facts, problems, and games in this book, you are officially certified as a graphs and statistics master! Make a photocopy of this certificate, write your name on the copy, and hang it on the wall.

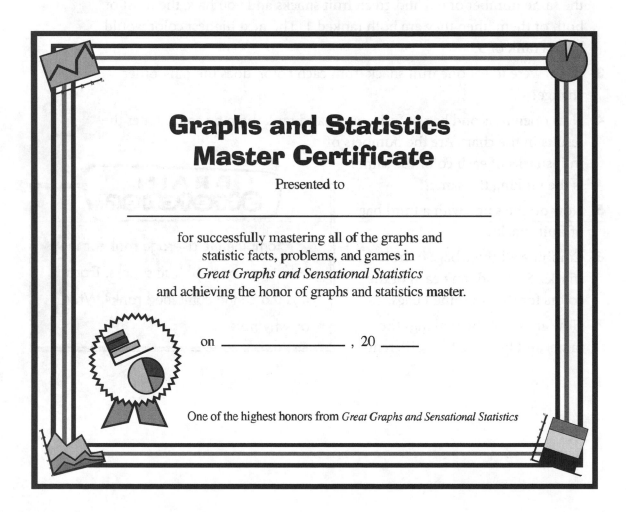

Graphs and Statistics Master Certificate

Presented to

_____

for successfully mastering all of the graphs and
statistic facts, problems, and games in
Great Graphs and Sensational Statistics
and achieving the honor of graphs and statistics master.

on _____ , 20 _____

One of the highest honors from *Great Graphs and Sensational Statistics*

Index

average
    computing, 14, 70, 92
    description of, 1–2
    grade-point, computing,
        97–98

bar graphs
    ball bounces, 28–29
    chance and, 19–21
    Chinese zodiac and, 27
    choosing cards by, 22–23
    description of, 1, 17
    interpreting, 30–31
    items and continent where
        made, 74
    zodiac signs and, 24–26
basketball pictograph, 11–12

chance, computing, 10, 19–21
charts
    ball bounces, 28
    birthday and zodiac sign, 24
    birth month, 26
    calories from fat, 58
    color of fruit snacks, 114
    food, calories, and grams of
        fat, 57
    grades and points, 97
    growth in inches by day, 50
    items and country where
        made, 73

percentage and percentile,
    112
price of stock by day, 55
rolling dice, 19
scores and means, 96
tic-tac-toe results, 44
Tower Tallies game, 100, 101
trials at skill, 52
types of, 1
types of graphs in newspaper,
    82
vowel occurrences, 79
weight of babies, 108
    See also map charts; pie charts
Chinese zodiac, 27
collecting and organizing data,
    5–7
comparing
    graphs, 79–80
    statistics, 104–105
computing
    average, 14, 70, 92
    chance, 10, 19–21
    grade-point average, 97–98
    mean, 91–92, 93–94, 106
    median, 102–103
    mode, 99–101
    percentage, 7, 44, 111–113
    percentile, 111–113
    statistics, 6
curve, normal, 108–110

data
    collecting and organizing,
        5–7
    graphs and, 1
    interpreting graphs without,
        83–84
database, pie chart from, 40–42
double-line graphs, 57–59

estimating mean, 94–95

grade-point average, computing,
    97–98
Graphs and Statistics Master
    Certificate, 116
graphing words, creating word
    search game using, 86–87
graphs
    comparing, 79–80
    finding in newspaper,
        81–82
    interpreting without data,
        83–84
    normal curve, 108–110
    types of, 1
    See also bar graphs; line
        graphs; pictographs

high score, reporting, 106

interpreting
    bar graphs, 30–31
    graphs without data, 83–84
    pictographs, 13–14, 15–16
    pie charts, 45–46
    weather map, 75–76

line graphs
    calories and fat consumed,
        57–59
    description of, 1, 47
    diagrams and, 62–63
    double-line, 57–59
    improvement in skill,
        52–54
    inches versus days of growth,
        49–51
    price of stock, 55–56
    scores and means, 96
    three sets of data on one line,
        60–61
low score, reporting, 106

map charts
    constructing, 67–68
    description of, 1, 65
    interpreting, 75–76
    items and continent where
        made, 74
    items and country where
        made, 72–73
    mail origin, 69
    mail travel time, 70–71
mean
    comparing to mode and
        median, 104–105
    computing, 91–92, 93–94,
        106
    description of, 1–2
    estimating, 94–95
median
    comparing to mean and
        mode, 104–105

computing, 102–103
definition of, 102
mode
    comparing to mean and
      median, 104–105
    computing, 99–101
    definition of, 99

normal curve, 108–110

organizing data, 5–7

percentage, computing, 7, 44,
    111–113
percentile, computing, 111–113
pictographs
    basketball, 11–12
    collecting data for, 5–7
    creating and interpreting,
      13–14
    description of, 1, 3
    reading and answering ques-
      tions about, 15–16
    3-dimensional (3-D), 8–9
pie charts
    creating, 35–37
    from database, 40–42
    description of, 1, 33
    interpreting, 45–46
    probability and, 38–39
    tic-tac-toe results, 43–44

types of graphs in newspaper,
    82
postmark, 69, 70
probability, 38–39

range, reporting, 106
rank order, 114–115
reading pictographs, 15–16
reporting survey results, 106–107

statistics
    comparing, 104–105
    computing, 6
    description of, 1, 89
    median, computing, 102–103
    mode, computing, 99–101
    percentage, computing, 7
    See also average; mean
survey results
    graphing, 30–31, 32
    reporting, 106–107

3-dimensional (3-D) pictographs,
    8–9

weather map, interpreting,
    75–76
word search game, creating using
    graphing words, 86–87

zodiac signs, 25